D0573346

A RESOURCE HANDBOOK
FOR
SATIR CONCEPTS

A RESOURCE HANDBOOK
FOR
SATIR CONCEPTS

Compiled by Johanna Schwab

SCIENCE AND BEHAVIOR BOOKS, INC.
Palo Alto, California

Printed in the United States of America.

Library of Congress Card Number 90-062013

ISBN 8314-0073-0

Illustrations by Dick Davies and Lynn Marsh
Cover design by Lynn Marsh
Editing and Interior design by Rain Blockley
Typography by BookPrep

Contents

Preface

*"Every person wants to survive, to grow, to be productive,
to make sense and order, to be creative, and to get close to
others . . . I believe growth is possible for every living
person . . . I believe every person has the potential for
change."*

—Virginia Satir

This quotation is one of the many statements by Virginia Satir that describe her philosophy of hope and belief: her life work was its expression. It is what attracted people from many places throughout the world to learn from her, and to be able to use her concepts in their work and in their lives. I was one of the many who were inspired by her. Beginning in 1963 I attended many of her seminars and training workshops to learn and practice her approach. To deepen and clarify my understanding, I took careful notes and copied her charts and diagrams, which I have retained as reminders and references.

This book represents material I accumulated in my association with Virginia Satir over twenty-five years. My hope is that you find this collection of value in connection with your experiences with the Satir approach—whether from books, video- and audio-tapes, attendance at workshops and seminars, or following her concepts in your personal and professional life. The handbook is a reference that can serve to refresh your memory, add to your understandings, and encourage you to create and amplify your own ways of conceptualizing Satir constructs.

The handbook includes explanations, descriptions, charts, and diagrams of Satir theory, techniques, and tools. She believed that words alone are not sufficient to convey what we intend to communicate—especially in the learning context. Utilizing any method that offered a more complete understanding and clarification, she created distinctive and innovative ways to present her ideas and concepts.

Many of these diagrams, charts, and explanations date from the 1960s and are presented as I first experienced them. I have included them to show that despite the amplifications Satir made over the years to extend and clarify her concepts and beliefs, her basic approach remained constant. The form of her presentations varied; the essence of her belief, never.

Using the Resource Handbook

Use this handbook as a resource, an adjunct to the work you are doing that is based on Satir concepts, whether in experiential or didactic sessions, in supervision, or in training. These materials supplement the ideas presented in *The Satir Approach to Communication* (Schwab et al., 1989), *Step by Step* (Baldwin and Satir, 1987), and other books by and about Satir's work (see the Bibliography).

You are free to duplicate and give as handouts any of the material in the handbook when you want to emphasize a particular concept or idea. In your position as teacher, facilitator, therapist, or other people-helper, however, it is essential to use her material in a manner that attends to her basic principles:

- To be sure each person is comfortable
- To contact each person, to make a connection
- To establish an atmosphere of trust and safety
- To be sensitive to timing
- To respect each person and his or her feelings
- To continue to build and enhance people's self-esteem
- To build communication bridges that help people move comfortably from one situation to another
- To pay attention to the process of the communication

I.

THEORIES
AND
CONCEPTS

A Bare-Bones Overview

The Satir model is a dynamic, organic, humanistic, systems approach to growth. It integrates existing resources to transform and make realistic changes that go toward the empowerment, healing, and growth of the individual and the healthy functioning of his or her system. This system can be family, professional, social, or political.

Learning and changing are based on her
BELIEFS:

- That change is always possible
- That we have within us all the resources necessary for growth
- That any past learnings that are unsatisfactory and painful can be replaced with new learnings
- That learning occurs within a framework that is comfortable, warm, and nourishing
- That everything is subject to use as a resource
- That all behavior is an effort at growth
- That choices are decisions one makes at a moment in time
- That the primary triad—mother, father, child—represents the original ingredients for identity and has the potential for being a nourishing source of growth and energy

Recognizing that people share
BASIC NEEDS COMMON TO ALL:

To survive
To grow and learn
To be productive and creative
To make sense and order
To get close to others

That learning and changing happen when there is a
CONTEXT:

That is **HUMANISTIC** . . . . relating to people
DYNAMIC . . . . moving and changing
ORGANIC . . . . nonhierarchical
CREATIVE. . . . . allowing new possibilities, inputs, and copings

With an emphasis on increasing skills to have
CONGRUENT COMMUNICATION:

> To give, receive and check out information openly, clearly, directly
> To express one's needs appropriately

Noting that communication occurs at a
TIME and **PLACE**

And with a
PURPOSE,

Raising feelings of
SELF-ESTEEM:

- By seeing differentness as a channel for growth
- By reinforcing the uniqueness of each person
- By empowering and energizing each person
- By manifesting sexuality in ways that are fitting
- By making decisions based on reality rather than on who has the power
- By being in touch with one's resources.

RESULTING IN
LIVING THE FIVE FREEDOMS

"To say what one thinks, instead of what one should say
To see and hear what is there, instead of what one should
*   see and hear*
To feel what one feels, instead of how one should feel
To ask for what one wants, instead of waiting for
*   permission*
To take risks in one's behalf, instead of choosing to be
*   safe."*

—Virginia Satir

Communication

"We learned how to communicate from the designers of our lives; we are not necessarily stuck with those ways when they get in the way of a satisfying relationship."

—*Virginia Satir*

Virginia Satir firmly believed in the importance of understanding communication in all its aspects. She offered many ways to help people be sensitive to how they express themselves and to alter patterns that affect relationships adversely. The following pages as well as other sections of the handbook show some of these ways.

In the family, **communication** is learned by:

> WHAT we observe, see, and hear
> WHAT others do
> HOW others act, react, respond, and perform
> WHAT the rules are and how explicit or implicit they are
> WHAT is permitted to be said or done, whether tacitly or specifically

The kind of communication we use is influenced by our life situations, which also affect how we respond. Both personal and interpersonal situations and conditions exert this influence.

Personal factors are:

> Feelings
> Thoughts
> Body reactions
> The senses
> The state of physical health; any physical handicaps
> Prejudices and fantasies

Interpersonal factors are:

The rules: who speaks, when, how, and about what
Societal, spiritual, cultural values and restrictions
The environment
Expectations and yearnings
Assumptions
Past experiences
Current realities
Conclusions
Stereotypes
Survival shadows

Communication and Self-Esteem

"The way we talk to another can affect how we feel about ourselves, how we feel about the other person. Self-esteem allows for choosing behaviors in a state of awareness."

—*Virginia Satir*

How we "talk"

AFFECTS

Our feelings about ourselves
and
Our feelings about others

which

AFFECT

How we "talk"
and
What we "say"
and
Our "conclusions"
and
Our "behavior"

which

AFFECT

Our feelings about ourselves
and
Our feelings about others

which

TOGETHER AFFECT

Our level of self-esteem.

A Communication Transaction

"What a person says at a moment in time represents his or her truth as he or she sees it at that moment . . . Any statement, question, report contains at least two things: my perception of myself and my expectations of the other person."

—*Virginia Satir*

WHEN I want to say something
WHAT I intend to say, want to say, and actually say

ARE SIFTED THROUGH

My thoughts, feelings, senses, conclusions,
The state of my physical being,
My current reality, past experiences, and
All my other communication filters

WHICH DETERMINE

WHAT I do actually say and
HOW I look and act
Which is communicated both verbally and nonverbally
as my message or report to you

WHICH YOU PERCEIVE

Through your senses and
Your communication filters

Your RESPONSE and your REACTION

ARE SIFTED THROUGH

Your thoughts, feelings, senses, conclusions,
The state of your physical being,
Your current reality, past experiences, and
All your other communication filters

Resulting in an **OUTCOME**
an **INTERACTION**
between YOU and ME

9

Filters that Affect, Alter, or Influence Communication

"Communication is a didactic process for making meaning; the variables are words, voice, and tone. Those are the things that affect the process. . . ."

—*Virginia Satir*

DIFFERING BODY POSITIONS
CHANGES in the NUMBERS of persons, or situations
FAMILY, CULTURAL, SOCIETAL, RELIGIOUS RULES
MAKING PLANS and DECISIONS; having to CONFORM
SEPARATIONS
RISKS
INTERRUPTIONS, INCLUSIONS, EXCLUSIONS
ENTERING A NEW SITUATION or leaving an ONGOING SITUATION
FEELINGS of the PHYSICAL BODY RESPONSES to fear, loss, frustration, helplessness, impotence, anger, pain, resentment, etc.
MAKING ASSUMPTIONS and HAVING PREJUDICES
HEARING GOSSIP and RUMORS
SELF/OTHER/CONTEXT DILEMMA
TIMING DILEMMAS
DIFFERING PERCEPTIONS of an event, behavior, or statement

Content and Process

*"You can't change the content of a problem—that is
outside of us. What you can change is the process of coping
. . . 'process' is arrived at through something in the
'content' . . . no matter the situation, the way in which you
handle the processes around it will determine the use of
that experience, this is where growth comes in."*

—*Virginia Satir*

The concepts of "content" and "process" are difficult to explain with words. The
difference between process and content is unclear at times: they are actually two parts
of a whole. I use the following description to help distinguish these important
concepts. Giving a demonstration also helps.

Content

Content refers to those behaviors, situations, and issues that we talk about in the
present, although they may have happened in the past, are in the present, or might
happen in some future time.

Content can be verbal, nonverbal, and/or behavioral.

Content is specific. Any subject, behavior, or feeling can be talked about: can be
described, explained, and interpreted. We can discuss how it was used or what we felt
about it. We can discuss how those feelings are reflected, what the rules are for
handling the feeling, and how those rules affect behavior.

To switch our focus from content to process during any interaction, it is important to
be aware of timing and selection. Clues include when the content signals a vulnerability,
problem, overreaction, difficulty, dilemma, pain, discrepancy, misunderstanding,
incongruent communication, or unfulfilling outcome.

Process

Process is active. It is the message behind the message, the WHAT and HOW of each person's version of the content:

> WHAT it (the content) is, how it was seen and heard
> HOW it is explained
> EXPECTATIONS of what was desired
> CONCLUSIONS made
> FEELINGS involved
> RULES that judge the feelings or regulate how to handle and use them
> RESPONSES made
> COPINGS used

Process entails coping with people's feelings, especially those that have a survival value. These appear in times of stress and can contaminate the present with inappropriate emotional reactions or behavior. The root, the source, can be found somewhere in the past, usually when the person was very young. At that time some trauma or event produced a real feeling of helplessness, impotency, and powerlessness. Because of the person's age, literal survival was a real issue.

A survival feeling persists at some level and is usually out of awareness. It is aroused when a current situation raises similar feelings. It can also occur in situations that are similar to past ones. Either way the person will respond as if it were a present survival crisis, reacting with past feelings rather than recognizing present circumstances.

The task is to separate the past from the present so that even if a similar situation or feeling occurs, it will not contaminate the present and feelings about the present. However, it is important still to honor those vulnerable places, our survival feelings, which once helped us cope. Today we need to distinguish between when the survival feeling is a friend and when it is a trouble-maker.

Process also refers to how you allow, support, and empower people to get in touch with and access their own resources. From this position of increased self-esteem and empowerment, they can explore and find more fitting ways of coping with life and can live with more energy, creativity, and power.

EXAMPLE

During a session Iris talks about her father. She says she loves him and that they have a good relationship. The youngest of three children, she has been his favorite. For years, though, she gets a severe, incapacitating headache after speaking with him in person or by phone.

In this example, the content concerns Iris's relationship with her father. The clue to move from content to process is the discrepancy between her love for her father and the onset of her pain after contact with him. After checking for possible organic causes of these headaches, moving to process means exploring with Iris an understanding of the issues involved in this relationship and the derivation, meaning, and purpose that is served by her headaches.

Here are a few types of process questions that would help accomplish this.

> How does she see her relationship with her father now? When she was 10? 16? 21?
> What was good? Has that changed? When? How?
> What was bad? Has that changed? When? How?
> What are her feelings about the good part?
> What are her feelings about the bad or not-so-good part?
> How does she feel about being in touch with the bad or not-so-good part?
> What is it like for her as she goes beyond seeing only the good part ("One must always believe that a parent is all-good, all-kind") and becomes aware that her father has also acted in bad and disappointing ways?
> Is this something that has occurred at other times with other people in her life?

For therapist and client alike, this is one beginning of the process to understand how an outside manifestation and underlying forces relate. In this case, it emerged that Iris's headaches symbolically expressed the conflicts between her feelings (of dislike for her father) and her values ("I mustn't dislike him"). These conflicts resulted in painful and disconcerting confusion in her thinking (her head). Her pain represented the way she coped with the dislike she felt but could not acknowledge, even to herself. Her powerful mask of pain concealed the real and troubling issues of this and other relationships in her life.

For more information, you may also want to refer to the diagram that accompanies "Making Meaning of an Experience, Statement, or Behavior."

The Facilitator: The People-Helper

"The people-helper can only offer his or her resources, not demand they be accepted . . . your job as a therapist is to help people use their experiences for growth, and to find a way to integrate all of their experiences."

—Virginia Satir

The facilitator is one who consistently works in several areas:

In Communication

Promotes congruent communication
Provides alternatives and options for coping
Presents opportunities for raising feelings of self-worth
Encourages the participation of each person

In Enhancing Self-Esteem

Increases awareness of self and others
Is patient and realistic
Helps integrate past experiences and present conditions
Makes a person-to-person connection with each individual
Acknowledges and validates feelings
Offers dignity, trust, and respect to each person

In Use of Self

Models risk-taking and the freedom to comment
Energizes people
Creates an atmosphere for change
Uses lightness and humor, metaphors and imagery

Uses techniques appropriately

Uses his or her life experiences appropriately

Is alert to and explores survival-value situations and feelings and explores their roots and begins a reframing

Looks for meaning and understanding, not necessarily agreement

Has and uses knowledge of history, politics, literature, drama, psychology, biology, law, medicine, economics, sociology, physiology, and anthropology

Has and uses knowledge of theories of family systems, communication skills, and human development

Is open to further learning

Family Therapy

"What was not connected in the family of origin will be the basis of the contract in the present nuclear family."

—*Virginia Satir*

These comments can be useful as beginning statements when explaining and presenting an overview of family therapy.

The family is a system; its members are interdependent parts.

The system attempts to maintain a balance, even at the expense of creating individual pathology.

The identified patient (IP) metaphorically carries the family problems. If the IP is helped or cured, the pathology floats to another member.

A family is governed by rules and myths, on which interactions are patterned.

The family system can change and transform by dealing with its rules and myths.

The family therapist works with interactional, interpersonal, and intrapsychic material.

The family therapist assesses family functioning by considering these elements: the dynamics of the family system, the family structure, its communication patterns, and its ways of coping.

Family therapy can result in more effective coping, enhanced self-esteem, and healing of some narcissistic injuries. Changes can reduce chaos, help the family begin to function as a unit, get people's needs met (not at the expense of others), increase the self-esteem of its members, reduce sabotaging, and revise expectations while retaining yearnings.

Satir Theories About Families

"The family is where our world began, where we evolved our styles . . . The family prepares its members to take their place in the society, to become the nucleus of another family—to nurture, protect, and educate . . . Families are teachers of human beings, not the owner of human beings."

—Virginia Satir

THE SYSTEM is how the family copes with life, stress, and change.

> The system allows the family to function.
> A symptom is a "pain" that signals dysfunction in the system.
> The kind of signal—the symptom—gives clues, symbolically and
>   metaphorically, as to the nature of system, its rules, and its values.

THE RULES dictate whether the system is open or closed.

COMMUNICATION holds the system and the rules together; miscommunication indicates the existence of imbalance or snarls in the system.

THE FAMILY FUNCTIONS in these areas:

Communication	How are messages given, heard, and checked for meaning and clarity?
The uniqueness of each family member	How is uniqueness validated and manifested in self and others?
The existence of differences	Are sameness and differentness accepted? Is differentness used for growth, creativity, and new options?

The process of decision-making	Are decisions based on what fits rather than who has the power?
Power	Is power acknowledged, and is it used appropriately?
Sexuality	Is each member's manifestation of sexuality accepted and age-appropriate?

An Analysis of the Family System*

"Everything makes sense if you understand the premise."

—*Virginia Satir*

Each family can be analyzed in terms of its

> Outcomes
> Premise system
> Coding system
> Communication system
> Family members' functioning

These reflect the ways in which the adult male and female figures are managing the family.

The *outcomes* are what has happened in the family (as noted in the chronology and history) and how the family perceived and handled these events.

Premises include each member's perceptions of how events in the family happened, and how each member explains and interprets these events. They include the reactions of each member in relationship to him- or herself, to others, to outside objects, to his or her own growth, and to choices.

The *coding system* is defined as the specific words and the nonverbal language that a family uses to convey concepts and rules. Families have such rules for using or prohibiting certain ideas or behavior. These rules indicate the family's value system.

A family's *communication system* includes:

> The words, voice tones, pace, facial expressions, body reactions—all the ways information is given, received, and checked out

---

*Taken from the 1963–65 Joint Demonstration Project, Los Angeles Bureau of Public Assistance and Assistance League, Family Service Agency. Virginia Satir directed this program and trained both agencies' staffs.

The specificity, directness, clarity, and congruency of the words used
The way differences and uniqueness are validated and expressed
The way decisions and choices are made
The way power is used
The way sexuality is expressed

These indicate the family's typical communication pattern, how each member gets his or her needs met, and how each sees him- or herself as separate, unique, competent, and empowered.

A family's *functioning* is measured in its:

Communication: how messages get across
Social adaptation: how its members make room for others
Independence: how its members see themselves as individuals, how each sees him- or herself as different and as unique
Empowerment: how its members use power and energy

The Individual and the Family System

"The family faces in to the individual by teaching how to become human and faces out to the society by teaching values."

—*Virginia Satir*

The INDIVIDUAL has universal life needs:

> to survive
> to grow
> to be productive, creative
> to make sense and order
> to get close to others

which are met in

THE FAMILY, which handles and determines how these needs are met

through

THE FAMILY SYSTEM, whose processes of managing the family communication, decision-making, validating uniqueness, constructive use of differences

affect the level of the

SELF-ESTEEM of each family member.

The Family as the Treatment Unit

"I'd like to develop for you some thinking about the development of family therapy and the idea of working with the whole family. What I would like to get across is that at this point in time, working with the family as we do now is a natural kind of evolvement from what we have looked at over the years in order to understand human problems.

"Looking at the family as the unit of treatment from one aspect is the development of how we look at the behavior of people who are, after all, the components of the family; so everything you know about individual growth, development, management, intrapsychic conflict is essential. . . . Two more elements: the person reacts in terms of his or her internal self but is also reacting according to his or her relationship with others in the family.

"Where we are in family therapy today as far as causation is concerned—there is a place for the constellation, the environment, the intrapsychic operation, the interpersonal operation."

Virginia Satir explained family therapy in this way during the series of training programs she conducted bi-weekly throughout 1963–65 and in several of her seminars at Esalen. She continually emphasized that when the family system is out of order, symptomatic behavior signals distortion in its members' growth, family rules inhibit growth, and dislocation or rupture occurs.

"The label of symptom is useful as the ticket of admission into treatment. It will give you clues as to the way stress is handled in the system. It gives symbolic and indirect clues to the suppressing aspect in the system, clues to the roadblock in growing, and signals that the system is overtaxed."

Virginia Satir maintained her belief in the validity and soundness of using the family as the unit of treatment and was committed to its practice. She demonstrated this in her writings and her work with thousands of families in many areas of the world throughout her career.

Measurement Guides for the Growth of a Family*

"Growth comes from what fits, not from what should be."

—*Virginia Satir*

Communication

Each member of the family speaks for him- or herself.

Each member can comment openly, speak directly and specifically, ask for information, and give answers to questions.

Each member can use feedback as nonjudgmental information.

Role Expectations

Each member is aware of his or her role, which is appropriate to his or her age, sex, and physical and intellectual condition.

The role is subject to change in relation to the person's growth, needs, and capacities.

Individual Responsibility

Each member is in charge of him- or herself, to a degree that is appropriate to his or her development.

---

*This guide was formulated during the 1963-65 Joint Demonstration Project, Los Angeles Bureau of Public Assistance and Assistance League, Family Service Agency.

Each member is able to make his or her own decisions, which are appropriate to and fit the circumstances.

Each member can take risks on his or her own behalf.

Integrating Differences: Validating Uniqueness

The family's techniques for handling differences include recognition, understanding, accommodation, and cooperation. No member ignores or denies the existence of differences or tries to dominate others as means of handling differences. The uniqueness of each person is acknowledged.

Cohesion

Family members are supportive of each other, with no antagonistic coalitions or scapegoating operations.

Power

Power is used for the empowerment of each member, not for giving away nor for telling other people what to do.

Sexuality

The expressions of each family member's sexuality are appropriate to the age of the member and the situation.

Closeness

Expressions of closeness and connecting through words and touch are freely and easily given and received.

Family Goals

Each member is able to coordinate his or her efforts toward achieving realistic and socially valued family and societal goals. These are subject to change over time.

Helping People Grow: Thoughts by Virginia Satir

These quotations are from seminars, workshops, and training programs given by Virginia Satir. They date from 1963–88.

On Coping

Our feelings tell us where we are; our intellect tells us what to do; our learnings provide new options; our experiences check them out.

When rules keep us from saying what we feel and think, our transactions are affected.

We model what we've been exposed to.

On Growth

We all go toward growth, no matter how thorny.

Growth and creativity come from what fits, not what should be.

We assume that because people have lived a certain number of years, they have stopped growing.

On Helping Others

You "open" people by light, warmth, and evolving; not by force, power, or coercion.

One of our aims is to get more deeply in touch with how we use ourselves and to develop more ways of using ourselves more creatively for other people.

Nothing is so terrible it can't be looked at.

You're not in charge of other people. You are in charge of the process of change.

Negative things don't have to be handled negatively.

Being aware of what is, is different from judging how to use it.

There are no solutions to problems; only possibilities.

Each person carries his or her own resources within. The thing is to help people get in touch with these inner resources.

People learn best in a nourishing atmosphere of warmth, comfort, and trust. . . . I work at the level of nurturing.

Familiarity is more powerful than comfort.

I want to make: the abstract concrete
the hidden obvious
the covert overt
the implicit explicit.

A people-helper is a person of resource, not a judge, an arbiter, nor a value changer.

The hope of any people-helper is to assist others in the process of taking charge of themselves, which is literally to stand balanced on his or her two feet physically, emotionally, and intellectually.

The contract I make is one of discovery—not an agreement to reach a certain point.

Those of us who say "I help" carry our tools where we are and where we go:

with our heart, we feel
with our head, we think
with our body, we move
with our personhood, we connect
with our divinity, we tune in with all life force.

Whatever comes to us in therapy is as a result of the use of things. The point is always how one uses what is or what was—the use of things is the critical point.

Anything is fodder for the therapist.

Interventions

"We make interventions to clarify hurt and pain: these are some of the signals for intervening."

—*Virginia Satir*

Interventions can be made at the level of:

The communication

The system

The self-worth

Interventions are spoken with words that are:

Concrete
Explicit
Overt
Clear
Direct
Nonjudgmental
Congruent

Interventions are prompted through:

I. Communication

How information is given
How information is received
How information is checked out
Its clarity, directness, specificity, and congruence

II. The Existence of a Discrepancy

A discrepancy between: the words and the behavior
                         the verbal and the nonverbal
                         the words and the feelings

III. Self-Esteem

The feelings about the self
The feelings about those feelings

IV. The Rules

The rules of society and the family
The rules for handling feelings and communication

V. Feelings

Feelings that are expressed in the present, talked about as occurring in the past, or oriented toward the future.

VI. Feelings About the Feeling

The rules concerning whether a particular feeling is OK and is therefore OK to have, or is not OK and therefore one we shouldn't have.

VII. Dilemmas Concerning Issues of

Differentness
Uniqueness
Power
Sexuality
Expectations
Yearnings
Conclusions
Outcomes

Ruptures

"Any piece of behavior is an effort at growth ... Food, money, sex, and discipline discussions can create ruptures between people where ordinarily there is good will. The ruptures have to do with not having enough information."

—*Virginia Satir*

In any unit, whatever the label—family, group, class, etc.—a system exists so that the unit can carry on with its functions.

The elements of the system are:

      The ways people COMMUNICATE
      The RULES for handling the communication and the feelings
      The level of SELF-ESTEEM of the people involved

CONNECTIONS exist between:

      incongruent communication and rules
      and
      feelings of discomfort and a state of imbalance

      discomfort and imbalance
      and
      the rupture point

      the rupture point
      and
      the communication stress responses

      the communication stress responses
      and
      the presence of pain

the presence of pain
and
the symptom

The symptom is a visible, audible, verbal or nonverbal, and/or behavioral mani-festation. The symptom is the signal that the system is out of balance.

Self-Esteem

"Our self-concept comes in childhood from messages about how to treat me, how to treat others, and how I come to expect others to treat me."

—*Virginia Satir*

The following elements help indicate the level of a person's self-esteem.

Security

Being comfortable and safe with people and the environment, and knowing that you have people with whom you can share

Belongingness

Being a part of and participating in some significant group

Personhood

Knowing who you are, what your roles are, and being comfortable with yourself

Competence

Experiencing success in projects, and feeling satisfaction and pleasure for your part

Direction

Having goals, aims, options, and possibilities; and using your awareness of the differences between realities and dreams

The Steps to Learning

"Learning and growth are a never-ending process. . . .
Growth and learning can come from any situation or
experience, problem or crisis."

—Virginia Satir

Step One

A past learning has already been integrated and is in use in a current situation, the "status quo."

Step Two

A "foreign element" enters. This could be another person, a new idea, approach, need, learning, or change in pace.

Step Three

There is chaos, a disturbance and confusion, which is the time a new learning is introduced yet is unintegrated. The past way is no longer fitting nor appropriate.

Step Four

The new learning is being integrated.

Step Five

The integration, which has just been understood intellectually, is now being practiced and is starting to be put into use.

Step Six

There is a new "status quo" with the new learnings now being used comfortably.

The Symptom

*"The dysfunction in any member of a family is a symptom
of disorder in the family and is a signal for help . . . The
presence of conflicts (symptoms) is a message about
something that needs to happen."*

—Virginia Satir

Symptoms can be in the behavior, communication, or interaction of members in the system. The system can be personal, interpersonal, or social.

The symptom gives clues symbolically, metaphorically, and indirectly about what the roadblocks are in the system. The symptom also can indicate what the values are in the system.

The symptom indicates the members' coping difficulties and unrealistic expectations, and the labels that are placed on members.

The symptom is a signal to the facilitator/therapist/trainer about a place to make an intervention. It does not give direction as to how it is to be treated.

Symptomatic behavior fits and has a purpose. Since it does not fit the time, purpose, person, or the context in which it occurs, it is necessary to explore what its meaning and function are.

II.

VISUAL PRESENTATIONS

CHARTS
DEMONSTRATIONS
DIAGRAMS

"Exercises help us become enlightened of life processes, to become aware."

—*Virginia Satir*

The Can of Worms

"Every person has his or her own perception of what happened . . . each picture is valid though it may not be the whole picture. Each person's picture needs to be seen, heard, and understood."

—*Virginia Satir*

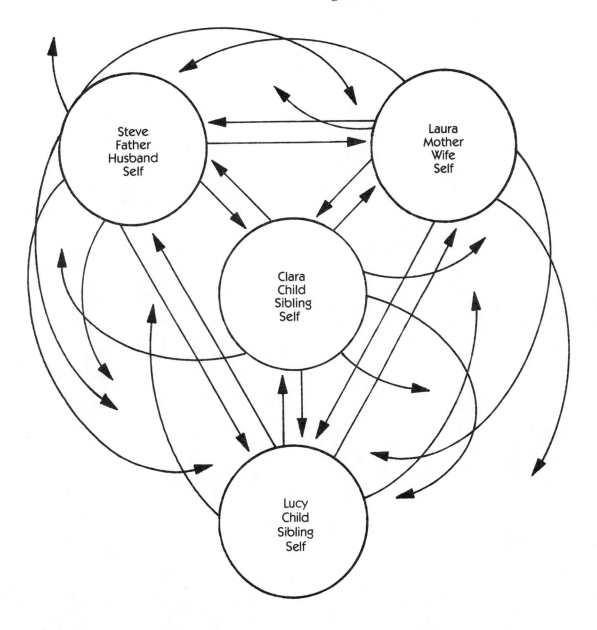

Each person in a family relates and responds from one of his or her many roles at any one point in time. It's crucial to know who is talking and in which role, who is listening and in which role, and who is observing and in which role. The chart illustrates this complexity and shows how communication snarls can occur, even with the best of intentions. Without recognizing this situation, we respond inappropriately— "If I speak to my husband, who is in his spouse role, and at this moment I am in my role of daughter of my mother, our communication interaction will be skewed." The outcome of these interactions is affected more by the communication than the content itself.

The Can of Worms Extended

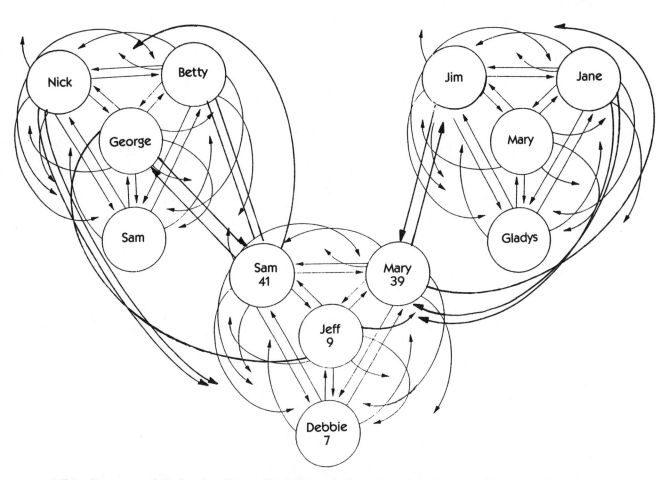

This diagram adds the families of origin to the nuclear family can-of-worms diagram. It is used to illustrate that questions can be extended to include the perceptions of any family member about other family-of-origin members whether living or dead, present or absent. For instance, you might say to the father in the nuclear family: "In your experience of having had brothers in your growing up, what did you learn that you can now use to help your two sons get along? What did you learn from your father about how to handle differences between children?"

Or you might say to the mother: "In your growing up as a daughter to a mother who had that same problem, how do you think you as a mother can now find other ways to make life better for you than it was for your mother?" Or to a son: "As the oldest son with two sisters, what do you think it was like for your father, being the oldest son in his family and also having two sisters? Is this something that would be of use for you in your family now?"

Crisis

The Chinese word for "crisis" is composed of two calligraphic characters as illustrated below. This is useful when there is a crisis and you want to give people another perspective: that a crisis has both positive and negative parts, and that each is valid.

The Ingredients of an Interaction

"I teach my students that this kind of an anatomy is an essential piece of knowledge that helps us to understand any piece of behavior. . . . I consider it to be the basic. . . . I have evolved questions which make it possible to get these pieces so that I can understand a piece of behavior."

—Virginia Satir

Virginia Satir had been evolving these concepts since the early 1960s, when she called this "the anatomy of an interaction." She presented this particular chart at a month-long seminar in 1970.

I. TWO PERSONS

interacting: each has a name, an age, and a gender identity

II. THE CONTEXT

This place—here
This time—now
Purpose—what
The situation
The expectations—hopes and fears
The contract
The role

III. THE RECEPTORS

Eyes
Ears
Nose
Mouth
Skin

IV. THE MANIFESTATIONS

Facial expressions
Muscle tone
Scent
Voice tone
Gestures

Body position
Skin color
Breathing
Movements
Words

V. INNER SPACE TRAVEL

Stored knowledge	Sensory input
Present information	Thoughts
Present awareness	Feelings
Past experiences	Body responses
Shadows	Survival rules

The conclusions

VI. THE RESPONSE

by the other person to the interaction
which is in words and/or behavior

All of these elements are present in any interaction between two people. They may not be evident or in awareness, yet each one affects what happens when two people interact.

Satir said the main components are the dyad, those two people's expectations for a joint outcome, and the time and place of the interaction. Altogether, she identified these fifteen parts as being applicable to any encounter between two people:

1. The request or need for an outcome
2. Two people
3. A specific time and place
4. The identity of each person
5. The conclusion of the self-other dilemma
6. The role label of each person
7. The contract they have made, implied, or assumed
8. The intrapsychic (feelings and thoughts)
9. The manifestations (voice, tone, face, body language, etc.), which are clues to what's going on inside each person
10. The discrepancy factor (the space between what one person intends and what the other one hears or sees)
11. The sensory receptors
12. Emotional limiters of the sense organs
13. Physical limiters
14. Rules for reporting
15. The matching of the manifestations of both people, and what happens when there is no matching

Making Meaning of an Experience, Statement, or Behavior

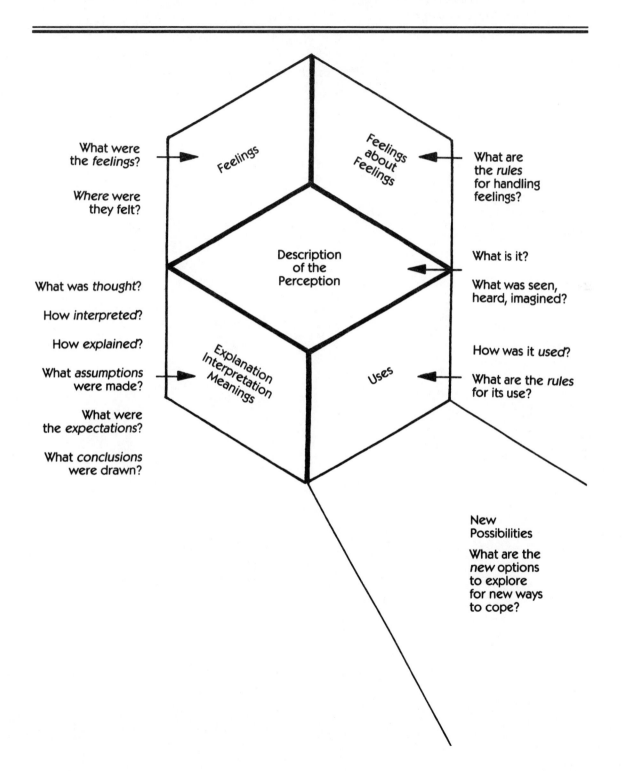

What were the *feelings*?

Where were they felt?

Feelings

Feelings about Feelings

What are the *rules* for handling feelings?

Description of the Perception

What is it?

What was seen, heard, imagined?

What was *thought*?

How *interpreted*?

How *explained*?

What *assumptions* were made?

What were the *expectations*?

What *conclusions* were drawn?

Explanation Interpretation Meanings

Uses

How was it *used*?

What are the *rules* for its use?

New Possibilities

What are the *new* options to explore for new ways to cope?

Mapping the Family Chronology

"This is not a history of what went bad or what went good, but an effort to get at the very thing of the development, the evolution of the family. If you look at the development of the family, you begin to see how the system balance is going. One of the ways that I try to put it in some organized way so that I can begin to get clues for the system is by taking the family chronology. I keep a chronological picture of who moves in and who moves out, and what happened at the point of natural crisis. When changes are made, whether they are changes that saw pain or discomfort, there has to be a way in which they are integrated.

"I keep track of it by the calendar and this gives me some pretty good clues as to the kind of system that is operating, by seeing the outcomes. Then, when I want to find out the whole perceptual aspect, I ask each person what happened, and get into the explanation, interpretation, and application. I do that as I'm going along."

—Virginia Satir

The following family maps show the evolvement of a family over time. To complete the chronology takes four charts: the Nuclear Family and (one per spouse:) the Families of Origin, the Family Cast of Characters, and the Circle of Influence.

Used together, these give a picture of the threads that weave and flow through the family generations: where the values stemmed from, where people learned how to be "human," where the family myths began.

Only verifiable facts are written on the maps. Included are:

    Names, nicknames, aliases
    Dates of birth, marriages, divorces, separations, remarriages, deaths, when the
        marital pair met

Dates of entrances into school and graduations; employment, educational, and military stints; and other significant events

Dates and identification of illnesses, traumas, dramatic occurrences, "Acts of God"

Dates of changes in residence, employment, etc.

The first chart, the Nuclear Family, diagrams all the people in the current family, living or dead, and whether or not they are all residing in the same home.

The next chart, the Families of Origin, shows all the people who are or were in the families of origin of the present family. It includes the parents and grandparents of each marital partner, together with siblings, mates, and children, and other marriages, if any. (The same can be done for a preceding generation if relevant.)

On both charts, in addition to dates and verifiable facts, include an adjective that describes each person and the stress response position he or she often took.

When creating these two charts, much of the time you will find that certain information is not known or available. Generally, the missing pieces can be approximated by using what is known, together with dates, places, events, and the world situation existing at that time. We are all human beings, and we have only so many ways available to respond to events. When we check them out later with actual facts, the pictures we create usually fall uncannily close to historical reality.

Examples on the following pages give some ideas how to compose the charts. Many times, however, there will be second marriages and blended families that complicate the diagrams, so be flexible in planning spaces for adding any additional information.

The third chart, the Family Cast of Characters, lists all persons—living or dead, present or absent, related or not—who have had a place in the family life history. This includes parents, grandparents, uncles, aunts, cousins, stepparents, children, persons from previous marriages, friends, teachers, clergy, and work associates. Everyone and everything can make a difference. This list also serves as a reminder of forgotten incidents and can indicate those persons who still are strangers and yet had or have a part in the family story.

The final chart, the Circle of Influence, diagrams those six, seven, or eight people who knew, nurtured, supported, and directed you at least up to the age of six.

To compose this chart, each family member draws a circle in the center of a page and puts his or her name in it. He or she draws other circles around it, putting names of those people in the center of each. If the significant person is no longer living, the family member draws lines to shade the circle. For anyone who was especially significant, whether for good or evil, have members make the line extra thick around the circle. And have them draw a squiggly line between their circle and the circle of any person who took care of them as a baby.

Next, family members each select adjectives for the people on their charts—an adjective that represents whatever meaning each person had. They write that adjective next to the circle that contains the person's name.

Finally, each member makes a list at the bottom of the page of all those adjectives that apply to him or her, and marks those that are acceptable versus those that are not. All these adjectives had a role in his or her curriculum for how to be a person.

The Circle of Influence is a vivid, visual way to illuminate the verbal and nonverbal messages a person received as a child to learn how to be "human." There is a special impact from these people: they were and are of significant importance to survival. The chart is a way to look at them now with grown-up eyes and determine which are still useful to life and which no longer fit.

The Nuclear Family

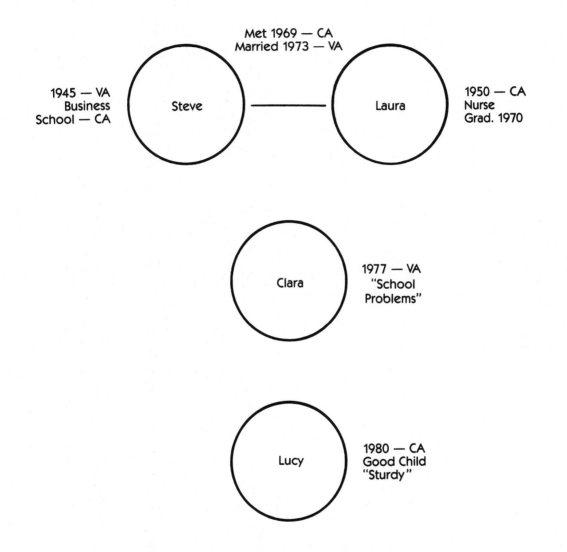

Met 1969 — CA
Married 1973 — VA

1945 — VA
Business
School — CA

Steve

Laura

1950 — CA
Nurse
Grad. 1970

Clara

1977 — VA
"School
Problems"

Lucy

1980 — CA
Good Child
"Sturdy"

Families of Origin:
Maternal Family

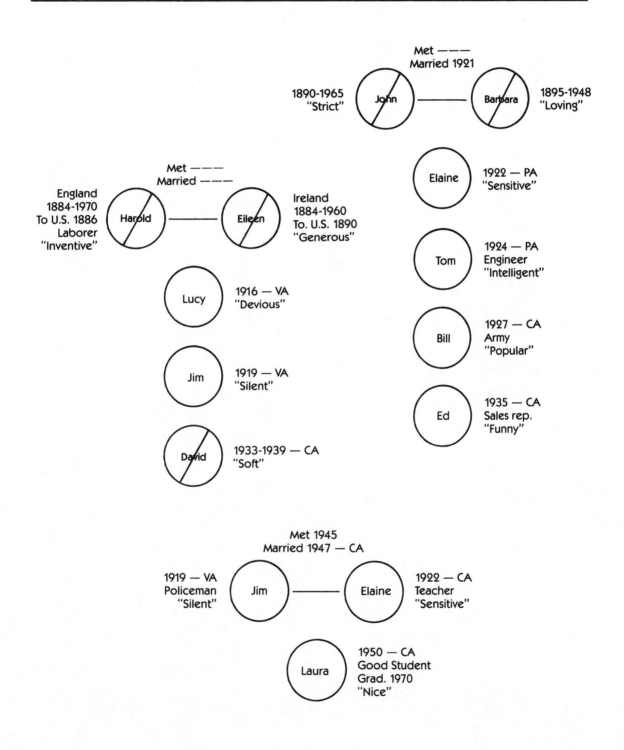

Met ———
Married 1921

1890-1965
"Strict"
John — Barbara
1895-1948
"Loving"

Met ———
Married ———

England
1884-1970
To U.S. 1886
Laborer
"Inventive"
Harold — Eileen
Ireland
1884-1960
To. U.S. 1890
"Generous"

Elaine 1922 — PA
"Sensitive"

Lucy 1916 — VA
"Devious"

Tom 1924 — PA
Engineer
"Intelligent"

Jim 1919 — VA
"Silent"

Bill 1927 — CA
Army
"Popular"

David 1933-1939 — CA
"Soft"

Ed 1935 — CA
Sales rep.
"Funny"

Met 1945
Married 1947 — CA

1919 — VA
Policeman
"Silent"
Jim — Elaine
1922 — CA
Teacher
"Sensitive"

Laura 1950 — CA
Good Student
Grad. 1970
"Nice"

Families of Origin: Paternal Family

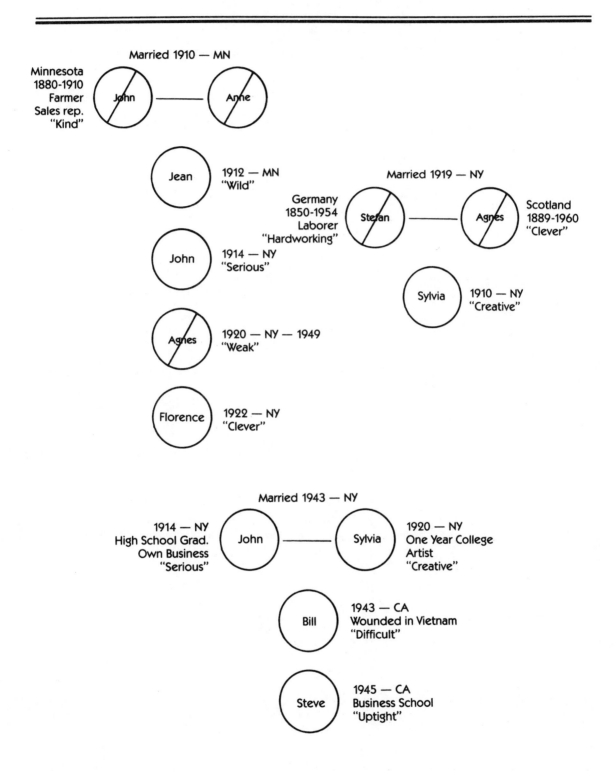

Married 1910 — MN

Minnesota
1880-1910
Farmer
Sales rep.
"Kind"

John — Anne

Jean
1912 — MN
"Wild"

Married 1919 — NY

Germany
1850-1954
Laborer
"Hardworking"

Stefan — Agnes

Scotland
1889-1960
"Clever"

John
1914 — NY
"Serious"

Sylvia
1910 — NY
"Creative"

Agnes
1920 — NY — 1949
"Weak"

Florence
1922 — NY
"Clever"

Married 1943 — NY

1914 — NY
High School Grad.
Own Business
"Serious"

John — Sylvia

1920 — NY
One Year College
Artist
"Creative"

Bill
1943 — CA
Wounded in Vietnam
"Difficult"

Steve
1945 — CA
Business School
"Uptight"

Family Cast of Characters:
Maternal Family

MALE			FEMALE		
Name	Current Age	Where Now	Name	Current Age	Where Now

Family Cast of Characters:
Paternal Family

MALE			FEMALE		
Name	Current Age	Where Now	Name	Current Age	Where Now

The Circle of Influence: Maternal Family

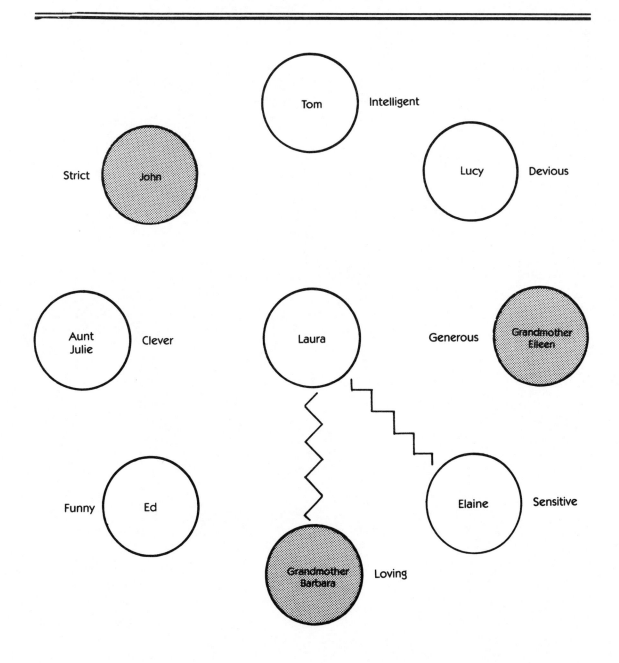

Intelligent (acceptable)
Strict (not acceptable)
Clever (acceptable)
Loving (acceptable)

The Circle of Influence: Paternal Family

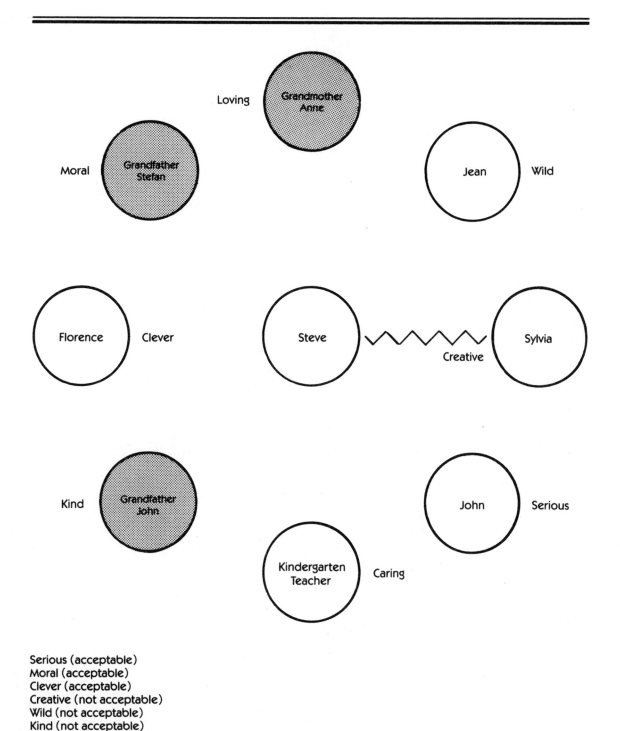

Serious (acceptable)
Moral (acceptable)
Clever (acceptable)
Creative (not acceptable)
Wild (not acceptable)
Kind (not acceptable)

Stress Responses and the Self/Other/Context Dilemma

"Every message contains at least three things: something about me, about you, and about the context."

—*Virginia Satir*

STRESS RESPONSE NUMBER ONE

In the self/other/context dilemma, this response counts out the self:

"I'm nothing without you."

"I can't live without you."

"It's all my fault, dear."

This person always uses words that:

agree
placate
accept all blame

This person is known as:

dependent
"too good"
the martyr
weak
infantile
a placater

STRESS RESPONSE
NUMBER TWO

In the self/other/context dilemma, this response counts out the other person:

"You need me to exist."

"It's always your fault."

This person always uses words that:

disagree
blame
find fault
judge

This person is known as:

hostile
a tyrant
a nag
difficult
"bossy"

STRESS RESPONSE
NUMBER THREE

In the self/other/context dilemma, this response counts out both self and other:

"One lives by the book."

This person always uses big words that tell you how one does things according to the experts.

This person is known as:

rigid
compulsive
an "egghead"
disciplined
an authority
principled

STRESS RESPONSE
NUMBER FOUR

In the self/other/context dilemma, this response counts out self, other, and the context:

"Does it really matter?"

This person uses words that are:

irrelevant
confusing

This person seems to be in constant motion.

This person is known as:

a distractor
inappropriate
hyperactive
capricious
eccentric

74

STRESS RESPONSE
NUMBER FIVE

In the self/other/context dilemma, this response counts all in: self, other, and the context.

"I want to share this particular time with you. Can you be with me now?"

This person uses words that are:

specific
congruent
fitting
ego-enhancing
direct

This person is known as:

creative
competent
productive
integrated
unique

A Description of the Stress Responses

POSITION	PERSON KNOWN AS	SELF, OTHER, CONTEXT
Number One		
Placating position	Dependent, martyr weak, placater, infantile, "too good"	Counts out the self
Uses words of agreement, accepts blame		"I can't live without you!"
Number Two		
Blaming position	Hostile, a tyrant, difficult, bossy	Counts out the other
Uses words that blame, find fault, judge, disagree		"If it weren't for you . . ."
Number Three		
Preaching position	Rigid, compulsive, super-reasonable, authoritative	Counts out both self and other
Uses big words that dictate how one "should" do things		
Number Four		
Distracting position	Hyperactive, irrelevant, in constant motion	Counts out: self, other, and the context
Uses words that confuse		
Number Five		
Position fits situation	Competent, creative congruent, integrated	Counts all in: self, other, and the context
Uses words that fit the entire situation		

The Basis of the
Congruent Response

Belief

That no matter the age, sex, race or physical condition,

ALL people want to:

> Survive
> Grow
> Be productive
> Be creative
> Make sense and order
> Be close to others

Position

When interacting with another, be

> Physically comfortable
> Face to face
> At eye level

When this is not readily possible, make adjustments or be aware that some discomfort exists that could be affecting the interaction.

Attending

Be conscious of and take into consideration input from all the senses:

Sight	Touch
Sound	Taste
Smell	The "sixth sense"

Making Meaning

Use words that fit the body expressions and behavior.

Check out that what was intended matches what was heard.

Clarify information; be specific as to the time, person, place, and reality of the message.

Give nonjudgmental, noncritical listening and feedback.

Sharing

Verbalize experiences, express feelings, and respond to others.

Connect with others on the basis of

> discovering similar human experiences, feelings, and responses
> discovering and appreciating differences.

Sameness leads to initial comfort.

Differences increase excitement and growth, and stimulate new interests and creative efforts.

Stress Responses Illustrated

NO. 1 RESPONSE

<u>AGREE</u>

PLACATE

**COUNTS
SELF
OUT**

**WORDS
THAT
DESCRIBE
PERSON
WHEN HE
USES THE
FOLLOWING
RESPONSE**

**WEAK
CLUTCHING
"GOOD ONE"
INFANTILE
DEPENDENT**

NO. 2 RESPONSE

<u>DISAGREE</u>

BLAME

**COUNTS
OTHER
OUT**

**WORDS
THAT
DESCRIBE**

**VIOLENT
HOSTILE
TYRANNICAL
NAGGING**

NO. 3 RESPONSE

SUPER-
REASONABLE

COMPUTER

WORDS
THAT
DESCRIBE

CORRECT
RIGID
PRINCIPLED
OBJECTIVE
OBSESSIVE
COMPULSIVE

COUNTS OUT
BOTH
SELF & OTHER

NO. 4 RESPONSE

IRRELEVANT

DISTRACTOR
(CONTINUAL MOVING)

WORDS
THAT
DESCRIBE

ERRATIC
INAPPROPRIATE
HYPERACTIVE
PURPOSELESS

COUNTS OUT
SELF, OTHER,
AND CONTEXT

REAL
FLOW
CONGRUENT

WORDS
THAT
DESCRIBE

ALIVE
CREATIVE
INTERGRATED
BEAUTIFUL
HEALTHY
UNIQUE
COMPETENT

COUNTS
ALL IN . . .
SELF
OTHER
CONTEXT

The Mandala

"Everything makes a difference."

—*Virginia Satir*

The mandala is one of the ways Virginia Satir demonstrated that many elements, inner and outer, affect a person's actions, behavior, thinking, and health. These are always present yet may not be showing, be in our awareness, or be acknowledged.

Each is important to the whole and needs to be acknowledged, considered, and explored, especially when considering difficult issues or dilemmas. At any one point in time, one or several are visible and obvious and in the foreground; others are in the background and may be ignored or overlooked.

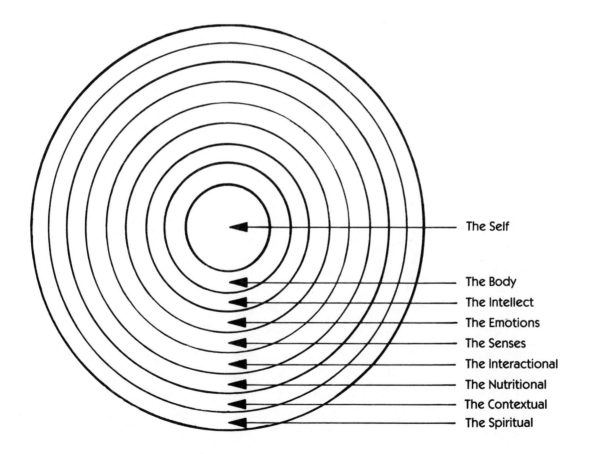

- The Self
- The Body
- The Intellect
- The Emotions
- The Senses
- The Interactional
- The Nutritional
- The Contextual
- The Spiritual

In working out your own mandala, draw a circle and then think of the different aspects or influences in your life, both internal and external. Your center is you, the inner circle. Then compose concentric circles around your center, making as many as there are aspects in your life. This gives you a way to observe how you coordinate them.

As you construct your mandala, be open to changing, adding, and deleting some circles. The mandala will give another picture of your life, the impact of each aspect on you, and each aspect's effect on the other parts of your life. It also presents a larger picture of how you relate to other people and their mandalas.

The Symptom and Its Function

"The dysfunction in any member of a family is a symptom of disorder in the family and is a signal for help."

—Virginia Satir

Imbalance in the system

Discomfort

Rupture point

Incongruent and ineffective coping

Pain

Manifestation of the symptom, the signal for change

Ways That Couples Relate

"When two people meet and begin a relationship, they now have to work out the 'us' part. How do you and I become 'us'?"

—*Virginia Satir*

Ask for two people to demonstrate these positions.

1. The couple is to stand back to back, locking arms. This pair presents two fronts and one backbone, which creates a static situation.

   The message: "We want to be connected and also related to the outside."

2. This pair stays connected by standing side by side, touching, and holding hands. This is a close-knit family, but it has trouble keeping in step while hanging on.

   The message: "We are sufficient unto each other forever."

3. The woman leans on the back of the man. There is one front, one back. There will be sexual difficulties and he will have back trouble.

   The message: "I am head of the house; the little lady is dependent."

4. This is like position 3 but with the partners changing roles. There will be sexual difficulties and she will have headaches.

   The message: "I am the head of the house; I make the decisions for us."

5. In this position the couple is together, sometimes holding hands, sometimes one leaning on the other, sometimes separating, free to be together, free to be apart.

Ways of Perceiving the World*

This format allows couples to experience their behavior patterns with each other: to recognize those that have negative effects, contrasted with those that are healthy.

HIERARCHICAL MODEL		ORGANIC-GROWTH MODEL
Symbol: **one up, one down**	THE DEFINITION OF A RELATIONSHIP	Symbol: **equality**
Feelings: fear, defensiveness, resentment, envy, isolation		People meet person to person.
Results: uses power to manipulate and dominate in order to feel potent		Results in feelings appropriate to the situation.

Symbol: a **box**	THE DEFINITION OF A PERSON	Symbol: **everyone is unique**
Leads to conformity, how you "should be."		Each person combines samenesses and differences.
To compensate, one must cut off feelings. Results in feelings of inadequacy, being judgmental.		

Symbol: a **line**	THE EXPLANATION FOR HOW EVENTS HAPPEN	Symbol: a **system**
Leads to seeing fixed answers.		What happens is a result of a system, a gestalt.
Results in stereotyping.		Results in looking for options and alternatives.

*Virginia Satir presented this model at a meeting in Aspen, Colorado in 1978. It became a significant part of many of her later lectures and seminars.

Symbol: **a stop sign**

Leads to a denial of change.

Results in fatigue, decay, tiredness because security is a way to keep the status quo.

Symbol: **closed system**

THE
ATTITUDE TOWARD
CHANGE

Symbol: **an open hand**

Leads to taking risks.

Results in having increased energy, use of new possibilities, creativity.

Symbol: **open system**

III.

TOOLS AND TECHNIQUES

"A tool or technique is only a way of going—it is not an end."

—Virginia Satir

Analyzing a Session or an Intervention

"We must permit interventions to be challenged and not treated as a subject for defense."

—*Virginia Satir*

This format is useful in analyzing your own work as well as in supervising others.

Documentation

Date, number of people, name of facilitator
Content: what is being talked about; or a behavior that occurred

Intervention Points

Discrepancies
Incongruent communication
Shadows*
Denial; avoidance of issues
Dilemmas
Unmet expectations
Presence of incongruent rules
Verbal or nonverbal expressions of feelings

---

*Shadows are situations from the past that intrude in a current situation because of some similarity—be it a same look, feeling, odor, event, or name—and affect the present.

Tools and Techniques Used

Connecting with people, making contact
Specifics: sculpting, temperature taking, rule transformation
Didactic material
The experience itself; role-playing; communication exercises
Dialoguing and discussion
Modeling
Humor
Generalizing, universalizing, reframing
Ego-enhancing questions and comments

Theme of the Session

What is the main issue?

The Meta-Message of a Statement or Response

What is the underlying statement, the unspoken part, the message behind the message, the issue behind the issue?

Areas That Were Covered in the Session

Bridging	Power
Expectations	Sexuality
The contract	Self-esteem
Changes	Yearnings
Comfort	Endings and closure
Communication	Separations
Uniqueness	Connecting
Differentness	Trust, dignity, respect
Decision-making	

Traps

Where were the places that were puzzling? What could be done differently?

Learnings

What could be learned from the experiences of the session?

Candle Lighting

"I can't light your light. I can only light mine so that I can illuminate for you to see to light your own light."

—Virginia Satir

For this experience you need matches and the short stubby candles that come in small glass containers. Have the room as dark as possible, and give each person a candle and matches.

The facilitator lights his or her candle with a match, then goes over to the next person so he or she can see enough to strike a match to light his or her candle.

Then the facilitator asks that everyone light only his or her own candle whenever they see well enough to strike a match.

When the group is a large one, only those nearest the facilitator will be able to see well enough to strike matches to light their candles. They then become the ones who illuminate the room sufficiently for others to see well enough to strike matches and light their candles.

This exercise is a metaphor for how learning and change occur without the therapist or teacher taking the responsibility for the learning of another. Virginia Satir often used this in her training programs to demonstrate that what she did was to make it possible for each person to be able to access their own energies and resources. In her words, *"I am not in charge of people . . . I am only in charge of the process of change."*

She gave a clear message to those who studied with her: that I cannot be dependent on another for my learning. Only I can be in charge of my own learning; others can merely show the way. Only I can take the steps to make a change.

Centering

"Tensions treated properly turn into energy."

—Virginia Satir

Centering is an important and convenient way to ground ourselves and others when beginning a new experience or when we feel anxiety, tension, or highly charged feelings. To continue with a new experience without taking care of the feelings present mitigates against our efforts to move ahead and restricts the potential for learning. Instead, our attention and energy are directed toward handling those feelings, rather than being attentive to the current situation.

First, acknowledge what is happening and comment on this before trying to deal with whatever was planned. Then ask everyone to close their eyes, make themselves comfortable, plant both feet firmly on the floor, and sit back in their chairs so that the buttocks and back are well supported. If appropriate, especially at the beginning or ending of a session, include quiet background music. Next, ask them to become aware of their breathing by placing a hand over the chest area, and to be in touch with the beating of the heart by placing their fingers on the pulse. Comment that without any thinking on our part, our bodies take care of all our life forces that maintain and support us. After a few moments of quiet, when ready, ask them to open their eyes slowly and look around the room without strain.

An alternative to this centering is to give a meditation, with or without music.

When as the leader you are feeling "out of sync" or "stuck" at any time during a session, let yourself be aware of this. You can share this with the group and then take a moment to use this exercise to center yourself. Or, take a moment to do this silently by yourself.

Communicating in a Triad

"It's not that I reject you, but rather it doesn't fit for me now . . . the starting point is to make this clear."

—*Virginia Satir*

This experience clarifies and helps people recognize what can occur when three people are together and want to be effective, creative, or productive, or simply want to relate with each other. The third person, who cannot be in direct eye contact with the other two at that moment in time, may feel excluded and left out. Other feelings, such as exclusion, abandonment, powerlessness, and helplessness may also emerge.

It also shows how to cope differently with these situations and use the support, energies, and resources of all three people and make sharing possible. (For example, mere body placement of the three people can lead to distressful feelings.) This exercise can clarify that being left out and feeling left out are separate and distinct— one a feeling, the other a reality. Just because you are the third person in a triangle, the intent of the others is not to leave you out unless they so indicate.

Have your group members divide into groups of three, make themselves comfortable, and select a letter each (either "A," "B," or "C"). "A" and "B" sit face to face and begin a conversation with "C" being the observer, saying nothing nor being addressed by the other members of the triad. After five minutes, "B" becomes the observer. After another five minutes, "C" becomes the observer. After each change or after all have had the experience of being the observer, they initiate a discussion of what it was like to be the observer, and what it was like to converse with a third person looking on.

For the next part, ask "A" and "B" to stand together, facing ahead. "C" stands behind, facing the backs of "A" and "B". This is to be done in silence for a half minute. Have people take turns standing behind. Next, ask that "C" try nonverbally to get between "A" and "B". Give each person a turn.

The final part is to ask that "A" and "B" vie, nonverbally, for the attention of "C." End with a discussion of what this and the entire experience was like.

Examples of Ego-Enhancing Questions

"What we say takes a direction, a course. If what we say is 'why,' all that can come out is research for cause and effect . . . When what comes out is 'how,' the 'how' can change the conditions that could make a change possible."

—*Virginia Satir*

About Communication

Let me see if I hear you. You want to have ---.

That's a new piece of information. How does this fit for you?

Can you offer something else?

Somehow you didn't find the joy and pleasure that you wanted and hoped for. How do you explain to yourself how that happened?

Is there something special about this that you don't understand?

Would it be OK for you to ask about that?

What I'm getting an impression of is ---. Is that your impression? How is it the same? How is it different?

Is there a question you want to ask now?

What does that mean to you today, what happened ten years ago?

How was it for you, being here today?

This is for my benefit, but would you tell that to him/her?

How can you say things about each other without playing a game and score-boarding it?

What would you like from him/her right now?

About Options

You now have some new possibilities. What are you aware of now that might change things?

Is this a possibility for you (for you and him/her)?

I notice that the atmosphere has changed, that there is some discomfort. Is that the same for you? What can you do to help change that?

Is there some other way of going? Not how bad or wrong he/she is, but how you'd like him/her to change?

Would you be willing to try something on for size?

You may not like this, but will you take a risk and see what happens?

How do you think it might go differently for you now?

About Feelings

What did that feel like for you to always feel that it's not possible?

Right now let me tell you how I'm feeling. How is that for you?

I've never known anyone who is 100 percent able to please everyone. How do you feel about hearing that?

Can you believe that it's not his/her intention? If you believe it, what parts don't you believe?

It's easy to misunderstand each other. How can you begin to believe that whenever something happens, it's not his/her intent, but due to something else?

When you thought about coming here today, what were your hopes, wishes?

Do you know some ways for how things could be different?

How does that feel, to contemplate that things could be different?

The Facilitator's Tools and Resources

"I start where I think I can start . . . Tools and techniques are only a way of going. They are not an end."

—Virginia Satir

Books, audiotapes and videotapes*

Exercises and experiences: communication exercises, response stances, sculpting

Information, life experiences, and insights from attending schools and universities, seminars and workshops

Specific techniques:

> Reframing
> Rules transformation
> Temperature reading
> Parts Party
> Mandala
> Family Reconstruction
> Mapping
> Ingredients of an Interaction
> Communication exercises
> Metaphors and imagery
> Generalizing statements
> Universalizing concepts
> Responding by seeing situations as "phenomena" rather than "problems"
> Using ego-enhancing words and questions
> Family life chronology

---

*For information on video- and audiotapes, write Avanta Network, 139 Forest Avenue, Palo Alto, CA 94301.

Use of yourself in making connections and contact:

       Your beliefs, warmth, humor
       Your general background knowledge
       Your specific knowledge of theories and techniques
       Your cultural background
       Your creativity and adaptability

Helping Others Make Changes

"Change is possible only in the present and when you get or give a new and different perspective . . . Taking in new information starts the process of change . . . From new use there is change . . . This is not easy: it is also a time to celebrate."

—Virginia Satir

Step One

The status quo—a plateau, a state of balance. The status quo is based on survival even though it may be nonproductive or symptomatic. The effort is to maintain balance even when the current way of doing things can no longer handle what is presently going on and there is some signal for the necessity for change. The feeling at this point is anxiety.

Step Two

The entry of a "foreign element"—in this case, a person from the outside (the therapist) comes in, which upsets the state of balance. The function of the "foreign element" in the helping situation is to deal with the effects of the imbalance and facilitate the change process. There can be some relief here by identifying "what is actually happening" and then making it manifest—articulating how it looks, sounds, feels, is used, and is experienced.

Note: The change and transformation process that Virginia Satir outlined in these steps was integral to her work with individuals, families, and trainees.

Step Three

Chaos. People begin exploring new options. Any new way is unintegrated while the old is no longer fitting, so there is distress and continued imbalance. The possibilities for new learning and change are greatest at this stage. This is where the competence of the facilitator emerges to make explicit the "context" of the old coping and to give the opportunity to develop the freedom to talk and to explore the options for other ways of coping. People feel more relief.

Step Four

A new perspective. There is more clarity about new possibilities and new options. This is when the integration of the new idea occurs, and when growth takes place and can continue. Each person begins to see him- or herself as a unique, differentiated self who can share and negotiate with others.

Step Five

Support. It is important that there is support and practice of the new ideas so that they become fully integrated.

Step Six

A new status quo. A new plateau or status quo is achieved and feelings of excitement are present as the new state of balance is reached.

Homework

For furthering your own development, here are some suggestions. Also, these can be useful in helping others learn, whether they be families, groups, or individuals.

Make a list of words that increase your vocabulary for expressing feelings (use the thesaurus).

Compose questions that are ego-enhancing.

Compose responses that are ego-enhancing.

Practice ways to make direct, personal connections with another person.

Increase your repertoire of metaphors.

Make your Family Map, Family Cast of Characters, and Circle of Influence.

Construct a "Temperature Taking" chart for home use.

Practice finding at least three different options when making decisions or resolving puzzles.

"I" Messages:
A Communication Exercise

"You need to put words to the obvious."

—Virginia Satir

Ask two people to face each other and to begin a conversation that has some meaning for both. Each person takes a turn responding to the conversation in the following structured way:

I feel [confused] that you are feeling [upset].

What I have learned about me is that [I need to check out with you before assuming that you are really feeling upset].

What I have learned about you is [that you are reluctant to talk about what bothers you].

I have had the opportunity to understand this about me: that [I have a hard time asking someone when it seems they are feeling bad].

What I will try to understand about you is that [you are careful not to hurt others and will not tell people what's going on].

The Parts Party

"How we deal with our parts is the essence of self-care. We can't love our parts until we find a way to use them."

—*Virginia Satir*

This format offers the experience of focusing on my feelings and thoughts about me and about you in a simple, direct, clear way.

The Objective

A Parts Party is an experiential technique that brings into awareness the different parts of ourselves. It helps a person to see the past from a new perspective, access resources, and create an atmosphere for change. Since many of our parts are unused, overused, misused, or ignored, a Parts Party introduces each part to the others. It also evolves ways of integrating the parts so they can cooperate in the interest of bettering relationships, ways of living, and ways of responding to life situations. The end of the party finds the parts coming together as a unit to resolve an issue, with the person recognizing and accepting ownership of all his or her parts.

The party can be held as a part of a seminar or in a group. The person having the party is the "host," and the facilitator is the "guide." Participants play the different parts. It is also possible to give a Parts Party when working with one person; that method is described below. The objectives are the same.

A Parts Party may take from two hours to half a day.

Preparation

The host is asked to consider the names of six to eight people who are well known in history, politics, literature, drama, television, or government. These people can be living or dead, real or fictional. The host selects half of the people for their positive qualities, the other half for their negative ones.

After the people have been selected, the host makes a list and writes one adjective after each name. These best describe the way he or she feels about those people or the meaning each one holds—why he or she was chosen.

The host asks different participants if they are willing to play his or her parts. If they accept, the host identifies them with the selected adjective: for instance, "you are my Einstein; you are my intelligence." To identify the parts, signs can be made to hang around people's necks or they can search for items to wear and props that indicate who they are.

Method

The guide discusses with the host the particular issue he or she wishes to explore, the reasons for wanting a Parts Party. Then the host decides the day, time, and place where the party is to be held. The guide explains that all the guests have been invited and all will attend.

Guests may enter the party one at a time or in groups and interact according to their roles and adjectives. The guide tells the parts to talk, respond, act in character, dramatize, and exaggerate their adjectives. The host and guide observe from the sidelines. Each time there is a cluster of people, whether because of a conflict, chaos, or misunderstanding, the guide freezes the action and simply points out to the host which part is with whom and what is happening, and asks what the host is experiencing.

The guide stays next to the host during the entire party, to be supportive and to watch for his or her reactions. The guide carefully observes what the parts are doing and saying that is significant, stopping the action when such an interaction occurs. At that time, the guide asks the host to pay attention to what has occurred and to ask what meaning that may have for him or her. Other times, the guide may check out what the host is aware of seeing and hearing. It is not necessary that the host respond verbally at any or all of these times. The guide asks that the host be in touch with whatever feelings may be present. The guide makes no interpretations.

After stopping the action and commenting, the guide asks the parts to resume their interactions. Whenever it is important to look more deeply at what is taking place, the guide again stops and freezes the action. At times, the guide asks the parts to intensify or exaggerate their characters to bring the dialogue and activity more clearly into focus. The guide can also ask the parts what they are attempting to do and, at another time, what they need to do to make the party more harmonious.

Depending on what fits, the guide may ask the host to direct the parts to make something happen. This indicates to the host that in reality, he or she is in control of his or her parts.

The guide may also ask the host to reframe the adjective of one or more parts from a negative to a positive, constructive one. "Stubborn" may change to "persevering"; "judgmental," to "discriminating." Sometimes this happens spontaneously, with the part making that transformation while playing the character.

When the guide believes that there is a resolution, he or she checks this with the host, asking how he or she feels about what is now happening and whether this is a good time to stop.

The guide asks the parts to form a circle around the host and then to sidestep so that each one faces the host directly, one at a time. The host tells each part the meaning that that part has had in his or her life, and now can have. Or each part, when directly in front of the host, identifies the adjective he or she represents and how he or she is or can be used by the host. After each part has spoken, the guide asks the host if he or she will accept owning that particular part. The host responds, "I accept you," if that is the case.

Finally the host turns and faces each part directly for a few seconds. The parts lightly and gently place their hands on the host's shoulder. After a few moments, they gently withdraw their hands, leaving the host standing alone.

The guide debriefs the parts before asking for feedback from the host, the parts, and the observers. This is an important part of the experience, to hear the personal impact of the host on the parts, the parts on the host, and on the observers. The experience is generally one that affects and has significance for all involved.

Variation

It is possible to have a Parts Party with one person whether or not he or she has had a group Parts Party. This technique is especially useful when the person has a dilemma or conflict, or is in a stuck place. (If the host has had a Parts Party, ask him or her to recall the parts that seem relevant to the current issue.)

Use the same preliminary procedure except ask the host to write each name selected and its adjective both on an index card and on another small, round card. The guide keeps the index cards; the host uses the round cards.

Place a large sheet of colored paper on the floor to represent the party room. Use the round cards to move the parts around as they enter, get together with other parts, separate, or move in or out of interacting. (Or use chess pieces instead of cards. To identify them, use tags with their names and adjectives.)

Proceed with the party, with you as the guide and the person as the host. Both of you play all parts, changing as necessary. Both create lines of dialogue, act them out, and direct the action. At any point either of you can be any part, the writer, or the director. This depends on the creativity of both the guide and the host.

Working on the current issue, the parts are to discuss among themselves how they can be helpful. The parts offer support by distancing, adding their perceptions and resources. For instance, Einstein may say, "I am here to help with my intelligence, which is needed to resolve this issue. I think I need to ask Woody Allen to add some lightness to the situation." Columbus could interrupt and add, "I think you also need my risk-taking ability."

You end this party when all the parts have offered their insights and resources, and the host is satisfied that he or she has received options for coping with the particular dilemma.

Sculpting

*"What is important is the image and discovering what it is . . .
There is an image behind the words."*

—Virginia Satir

Sculpting can be used in many situations:

> When unclear communication exists or unclear issues have not been satis-
> factorily clarified or integrated
> When people are at a "stuck" place
> When you want to illustrate a condition, situation, or event
> When you want to simulate an experience by role-playing
> When you want something less threatening than a verbal exchange for dealing
> with an issue that arouses intense reactions

At times, sculpting involves using the stress responses, and it's necessary to check out if everyone understands the stress responses. With those unfamiliar with the responses, it's essential to explain them, the words that accompany them, and to demonstrate their physical body positions.

In whatever way you will be using sculpting, it is important to first ask if the person or persons are willing to try something that may seem unusual but may be helpful in defining the issue.

One way is to have people assume the stress positions they had at the time when the disturbing event occurred. You can set up a sculpture or designate someone already involved in a situation to do so. When this is done, ask that each person say how he or she is feeling, both physically and emotionally; next, what he or she is feeling about the others. After which, have each person take a turn and alter the sculpture to reflect how he or she would want it to be. Again, ask each person how he or she is feeling.

Another effective use of sculpting is when a person is being pulled by having to make a choice between two alternatives. Ask for two volunteers, have each take one arm of the "pulled" person, and have them pull gently so there will be a physical sensation. (It is also possible to demonstrate pulls by using ropes: tie one around the waist of the person like a belt, and tie two others on opposite ends of the belt. Then have two volunteers pull on the rope.) When the person reports discomfort, ask the volunteers to relax their pulls. At that point, ask questions about the experience: the pain, where it was felt, and whether this feeling is a familiar one, resembling that when having to make a choice.

Ask the volunteers again to pull gently and to stop as the person begins again to feel some discomfort. Then inquire what and how he or she could do something to make him- or herself comfortable, and ask the person to do that.

Sculpting can be used to demonstrate our many roles: gender, professional, marital, social, familial, and so on. Provide a number of hats for each person. Identify each hat with a role, make a label for each role, and put one label on each hat. Place each person's hats one on top of the other. This dramatically shows the significance of the many roles each of us possesses. In which role are we behaving, responding, or presenting at a moment in time? And in which role do others see us at a moment in time?

The demonstration can be varied by asking people to converse from their different roles and to identify their roles by using their hats. The experience creates productive and creative discussions.

The Stress Ballet

*"I make pictures to allow the possibility that this view is
not the only view . . . to get unstuck [from the idea] that
there is only one specific picture."*

—*Virginia Satir*

This experience can be used as a demonstration with a family or group who is dealing with an issue that could be clarified by a visual, experiential presentation. (The words "family" and "family members" in this description can be replaced when some group other than a family engages in the experience.)

Ask that one member sculpt the picture that occurs when there is a rupture in the family. As the "sculptor," he or she arranges each family member in a stress response position according to how the sculptor sees the family's response to stress. Each other family member then takes a turn showing his or her own picture. (If people are not already familiar with the stress responses, you need to teach them.)

As each picture is made, ask the sculptor if that is exactly how he or she means it to be. If not, ask that changes be made. Then ask how it felt to be the sculptor. Finally, ask how each person in the picture feels about being in that position.

After each person has had a turn, ask for feedback from the members and from the observers.

For the next part the facilitator writes on a flip chart or blackboard the stress positions that were sculpted by each of the members. Next write a series of stress positions that each member is to follow, specifying different positions for each member. For instance, if the father was identified as being super-reasonable, he is to change from that to blaming, then being irrelevant, then placating. Mother may go from placating, to blaming, then to being super-reasonable; the child, from being irrelevant to placating, to blaming.

Ask the family to make their sculpture, beginning with the first position as written. Then ask each person to change to the next position as specified. Allow the family to remain in each position for a few moments until they feel the slightest physical discomfort. Ask that this all be done without talking.

After all the changes have been completed, ask that everyone freeze in the final position. Check out with each person how his or her body is feeling, what each is feeling about him- or herself, and how each is feeling about the other family members at that moment.

For the last request, ask each person to make only one move to make him- or herself more comfortable. Continue to ask that each person make other moves, one at a time, toward being more comfortable. When you see that everyone is in a comfortable position and relaxed, ask for feedback as to what they are experiencing now: physical sensations in their bodies as well as their feelings about the others. Have a general discussion about the entire experience with feedback from the observers.

Variation

Start a sequence as described above, except that before asking the family to move toward making themselves more comfortable, ask the following. In turn, each person, while taking one step at a time to make him- or herself comfortable, describes his or her physical condition and what he or she needs to achieve comfort. This may be something that he or she can do, or it may mean asking someone else to do something. This gives participants direct experience of using the Five Freedoms.

The Structured Interview

"Parents are people factories."

—*Virginia Satir*

This is a diagnostic tool developed by Virginia Satir, Don Jackson, and Paul Watzlawick at the Mental Research Institute during 1961-62. At that time, she used it in her teaching demonstrations when seeing a family for the first interview. She encouraged her students to use it as a diagnostic guide and to be better able to see elements of the family system in operation. As might be expected, Virginia herself gradually changed this rather strict format to an organic way of obtaining the same kind of information, covering the many areas that are specifically spelled out in the structured interview.

Today this structured interview is useful as a learning tool. It identifies the many parts of an interview that need to be considered in working with the family. Equally important are the implications and meanings of the material for understanding family dynamics, process, and system.

The description of the structured interview that follows uses the original format in both the order and the way questions are asked. After each answer, the interviewer gives no interpretation or response other than a "thank you." For each part of the interview, the interviewer keeps notes of the responses to the different questions and who made them.

Some of the original language has been changed. Words such as "problem" were replaced with others, such as "issue." "What would you like to change?" for "What would you like to have happen?" have also been added. The first question of the interview was changed to "What would you like to have happen as a result of being here today with your family?" These are the questions that Virginia used in her later work.

Two rooms are needed for the interview. The waiting room is used for the times when the counselor asks different members to go away and wait for the next part. The office, comfortably furnished, has seating arranged in a circle. Paper and pencils are needed for the written part of the interview.

Preparation

The discussion with the family member who makes the appointment includes the purpose of the interview, what to expect, and the need for spending two to three hours in the session. At the time of the interview, the family meets and gathers in the waiting room, where the interviewer greets them.

They are told that for the first part, each member will be asked individually to come into the interviewing room. The interviewer first asks the father, then mother, then the children from oldest to youngest.

Main Problem in the Family

The purpose of this part of the interview is to show what differences exist in each member's perception of the main problem in the family, and of what needs changing. In the usual context when seeing the family together, such a statement can be negative and potentially assaultive. In this context, it offers people the freedom to speak more openly.

This part exemplifies several concepts of family therapy:

- Each person sees the family problem differently; each person's perceptions are accurate for him or her.
- Each person has the right to speak.
- Each person is unique, as indicated here by the different interpretations.
- The way in which the problem is perceived offers clues about the communication and behavior rules in the family.
- What emerges is seeing the "problem" as the result of a dysfunctional system.

INDIVIDUAL INTERVIEWS

Each member comes into the office individually, according to age, and is asked: "What do you think is the main problem in the family at this time?" As each person leaves, he or she is asked not to discuss with the others what was talked about and to ask the next person to enter.

This part reveals:

- The problem areas in the family: whether it is the communication, behavior, distorted growth, or a syndrome of many problem areas
- Who receives negative energy
- How one person gives out information when seen without other family members, and what information he or she gives

FAMILY GROUP INTERVIEW

The last member to be seen individually is asked to invite the entire family into the office. The interviewer then asks: "Will you now together discuss what you think is the main problem in the family at this time? I will leave the room for a few minutes and when I return, I will ask what you have decided."

Upon returning to the room the interviewer asks: "Will you tell me what you have all decided is the main problem in this family at this time?"

This part reveals:

- The rules for commenting: who speaks, who is the family spokesperson, who responds, who speaks for whom, who responds for whom
- The manner in which the whole family is able to inquire into problems and to report them
- The private–public discrepancy: what is talked about when other members are present, as opposed to when each member is with the interviewer
- Any indication of rescue operations
- The presence of any coalitions, power struggles, and whether there is a devil–saint syndrome
- The places where people can converse and the places where there is silence or nonverbal communication
- How transactions are resolved, completed, altered, or left hanging

Planning

This section gives a picture of how the family system operates and the dyads within it. The interviewer asks the family: "Will you now together all plan something that you could enjoy doing together as a family? I will leave the room for a few minutes. When I return, will you tell me what you have planned to do together as a family?"

Returning, the interviewer asks: "What have you together decided that you as a family can do that you would all enjoy?"

Ensuing interaction makes possible a further analysis of the family communication—who speaks, who is silent, and in which groupings there is speech or silence.

This shows the existence of an overt–covert quotient: some of the dyads seemingly do not exist. They are not apparent and have had to go underground. In other words, a covert dyad exists between any two members who do not speak to or interact with each other.

This part of the interview also gives the first idea of how decisions in the family are arrived at—who gives, who takes.

There will usually be discussion among the family about the plans now being considered. Usually no plan has been totally agreed on. Despite this, the interview continues.

This part reveals:

- How the family functions as a unit
- Who takes the initiative and who compromises
- More indications of the family's communication pattern
- The quality of interactions and the differences that exist in the interactions of different dyads
- Differing needs, whose needs are met when there must be a choice
- More indicators about how decisions are reached
- The way power is handled and used, and which members have and use the power

Family groupings are next seen separately in the following order and asked:

With father and children (mother out of room): "What could you, [use name of father], plan to do together with [use names of all children] that you would all enjoy? And what could you, [use names of children], plan to do that you would enjoy doing with your father?"

Repeat the same question with each of the following groups, changing the names as appropriate:

Mother and children (father out of room)
Siblings (parents out of room)
Mother with each child separately
Father with each child separately
Males only
Females only
Marital pair

This part reveals:

- The way each member perceives his or her ability to survive and get validation of his or her self-concept
- Differences in how each is able to express his or her needs when the composition of the groupings changes
- When and in which groupings there are fewer ideas
- Which members disqualify themselves and their own wishes or plans

The First Meeting of the Marital Pair

This section presents the opportunity to see the marital pair as "man and woman, wife and husband," and to observe the quality of their interaction. The interviewer asks: "How did you two, of all the people in the world, get together?"

The wording of the question is specifically construed to imply that "you each are a person who could have made many choices," giving each a positive message of esteem and sense of self-worth.

Time is allowed for the story to be told by each.

This part reveals:

- Who takes charge, who speaks first
- Does one of the couple speak the majority of the time? Are there periods of silence? (If so, how do messages get across?)
- What were the relationship's original contract, intentions, and expectations? And what now are the disappointments?

Proverb

This section offers the opportunity to observe the operation of the couple in their roles as parents and teachers of their children. Each of the couple is given a slip of paper with the proverb: "A rolling stone gathers no moss."

The proverb presents a situation open to both literal and metaphorical interpretations. This is a paradox: neither part has more or less value than the other. However, most people make a choice. The result is usually a predictable disagreement as to which is the correct interpretation. This section presents the opportunity to see how the couple handles disagreements and how each maneuvers when their differences are not tolerated.

The interviewer asks: "Will you each think about the meaning of this proverb for a few minutes, then discuss the meaning between yourselves? Then plan how you can teach it to your children. I will leave the room for a few minutes. When I return, I will ask the children to come back into the room and then you will teach them what it means."

After not more than five minutes, the interviewer returns and asks the couple to invite the children back into the room and teach them the meaning of the proverb.

After the couple has finished the explanations, the interviewer asks each child in turn: "What do you think is the meaning of 'A rolling stone gathers no moss'?"

This part reveals:

- How the couple reaches a decision, if at all, and whether there is some agreement on how and what to teach
- Whether the paradox is seen and commented on, or if the parents become embroiled in a right-wrong bind
- Whether a single message is made, and whether what was taught matches what the couple agreed on
- The manner of the teaching (justification or explanation?)
- Whether there is a role discrepancy, with the parents asking the children to provide the answer
- The reactions of the children, and their freedom to ask questions for clarification

Main Fault and Main Asset

This part of the interview breaks family rules in a nonthreatening context. It indicates the negative values of the family. It allows family members to make statements in a safe environment about how each sees other family members. It also gives them the unusual opportunity to talk about their own positive qualities.

The interviewer asks: "Will you now seat yourselves clockwise according to your age: I will sit between [name of the oldest] and [name of the youngest]. Here are slips of paper and pencils. I would like each of you to write on one of them what you see as your own main fault. I will also write one." (Write "too good, too weak.")

The interviewer collects the slips, shuffles them (including the slip the interviewer has written), selects one, reads it, and then asks: "To whom do you think the words on this slip apply?"

The interviewer asks this question to each member in turn, and begins a list of the answers with the name of the person who made that answer. Each slip is handled in the same manner.

Then the interviewer asks: "Will you now write what you think is your own main assed? I will also write one." (Write "Always lets you know where he/she stands; always speaks out.")

The interviewer collects the slips, shuffles them as before, and follows the same procedure, asking "To whom do you think this one applies?"

Next, each person is asked to say, not write: "What do you admire most about the person on your left, and what do you admire most about yourself?" The person to the left of the interviewer is asked to begin.

This part reveals:

- What the family rules are about openly reporting what is seen, heard, or felt, and how easy or difficult it is to transcend those rules
- The value system of the family: what is "good," what is "bad," both the positive and negative values
- Any scapegoating, favoritism, or who gets blamed, by whom, and who blames him- or herself

Who Is in Charge of the Family?

This part indicates whether there is a leader in the family, who it is, whether the role is clear, or whether the children are in charge and parental leadership has been abdicated.

The interviewer asks each person, "Who do you think is in charge of this family?" Then the interviewer writes the answers and who made them.

This part reveals the nature of the leadership: static, authoritarian, changeable, or missing.

Sameness and Differentness

By making it evident that members can see themselves and each other differently in a different context, this part of the interview gives the opportunity to break stereotypes. It emphasizes that each member is a unique individual, and it specifies and identifies the sameness and differentness that exist in each person. However, because each person has his or her own combination of qualities, each is unique but related.

The father is asked: "Which of your children looks most like you, and which looks most like your wife?"

The mother is asked: "Which of your children looks most like you, and which looks most like your husband?"

Each child is asked: "Which of your parents do you think you are most like? How do you think you are different from your father, and how do you think you are different from your mother?"

The husband is asked: "How do you see yourself as different from your wife?"

The wife is asked: "How do you see yourself as different from your husband?"

This part reveals the ease or difficulty for each member to see him- or herself as separate and distinct from parents and siblings.

How Was This Experience?

This part offers the opportunity for the family members to express what the experience was like for each of them. It is an unstructured time for discussion. The feedback can reflect any differences that resulted from how the family members perceived themselves and each other at the beginning of the interview and now.

The discussion gives clues that can guide and assist the interviewer, who will be working with the family in their growth. The experience itself can be the onset of the process of change.

Each member is asked, in any order: "What was this like for you, [use name], to have had this time with [use names of all other family members]?"

The interviewer closes the session with whatever remarks he or she chooses that are appropriate to the situation, and thanks each one individually for coming and participating.

Temperature Reading

"Negative things don't have to be handled negatively . . . To transform a complaint is an opportunity to learn . . . The challenge is how to give feedback so it comes as a gift rather than as criticism."

—Virginia Satir

Temperature Reading is a practical, constructive way to help people check out and deal with the *what, why, when,* and *how* of their current life conditions. The purpose is to focus on what is or will be happening that needs attention or information. This is important as a way to circumvent the many problems of living together, be it in a family or a group, that arise simply because of a lack of information or a fear of asking for information.

This technique can be used daily, weekly, or periodically. Its format makes it possible to handle sensitive issues and achieve more positive, realistic results with few stressful feelings. There are several parts, all of which need not be covered each time. The order may be whichever way seems relevant at any particular time.

Information

What are each person's puzzles that need clarifying? Is there more information that needs presenting?

Complaints and Recommendations

What are each person's complaints, problems, or dilemmas? If there are any, what are the recommendations for solutions?

Worries and Concerns

Are there any worries or concerns and what are they?

Appreciations and Turn-ons

What appreciations or excitements do people want to share?

Wishes and Hopes

Does anyone have any wishes or hopes they want to express?

The Transformation of a Rule

"You can help people grow not by telling them that they are wrong, but by helping them transform rules."

—*Virginia Satir*

When a behavior or feeling seems to be in the way of a person talking more freely, there may be a "rule" present that is keeping the words in check. Rule transformation is highly useful and can be done any time during any session.

When you find that during an interview or session something is interfering with or influencing a response, suggest that a rule may be present and ask the person if he or she is willing to check it out. The person is usually unaware of any such rule, so you can encourage him or her to think of what it might be. The following words are present in rules and indicate that a person is responding more to a rule than to the reality of the present situation.

> always
> never
> should
> must
> ought

When necessary, restate this person's rule to make it more concise. Then check out whether that is what he or she intended; if not, continue changing the words until you and the person agree that the sentence contains exactly what he or she means. Modify it as many times as necessary and, after clarifying it, write the rule on the flip chart. Make a final check to make sure the written version means exactly what the person intends. Lastly, ask how he or she feels about seeing the written rule.

Next, in a step-by-step process, ask the person to add, delete, and/or substitute one or several words to form a new sentence. Here is an example.

Rule:	I must always be agreeable.
First change:	I must be agreeable. [Delete "always."]
Second change:	I can be agreeable. [Change the imperative to the possible.]
Third change:	I can be agreeable sometimes.

Write each revised sentence below the previous amended one, so that all changes are clearly visible.

The rules that create dilemmas contain words such as "always" or "must" because they impose immobility on thoughts and actions. They take no account of human factors. Harsh as a rule may be, however, something in it can be useful. To eliminate the entire rule and wipe it out of our mind and behavior is really not possible. What is possible is to transform it, maintaining its valid part and then creating a realistic statement that we can live with comfortably. The rigid rule thus becomes a valuable guideline.

The transformation process can end at any point where the person is comfortable, even if you see possibilities for further changes. In general, attempting to arrive at a complete transformation can be ill advised. The signal to stop is when you get feedback, verbal or nonverbal, that the person no longer wants further changes. (At a later date, after the person has adapted to these initial changes, you can comment that he or she may wish to go farther with the transformation of this rule.)

Using Virginia Satir Videotapes

*"The leader is a channel. . . . I give others ways and options
to go without damaging or injuring them."*

—*Virginia Satir*

Purpose

To experience Virginia Satir as she worked with families
To study her concepts of family therapy
To study her process and communication techniques
To study her ways of involving a group
To observe her use of self

The Elements of Process To Observe

Communication: Satir's clarity, directness, specificity, and congruence, and
how she dealt with the family's communication
Uniqueness: how she validated this in the individual family members
Differentness: how she acknowledged and underscored this in individual
family members
Power: how she empowered others
Sexuality: how she dealt with this
Self-Esteem: how she enhanced this
Connecting: how she made contact directly and indirectly
Decision-making: how she involved everyone in this process
Transformation: how she changed negative perceptions into positive uses
(e.g., "obstinate" to "persevering")

Suggestions on Presenting Satir Videotapes

Become familiar with the tape. Each one contains specific techniques and includes
basic concepts; some bring out certain concepts more than others. Being familiar with
the tape will make you more comfortable in its use.

Make an outline of the tapes you will be using and select the exact parts you want to use to illustrate a concept or a technique.

When reviewing a tape, make plans to stop whenever you wish to emphasize what Virginia did at that moment and for what reason.

Note the counter number on the tape machine where your selections begin and end; time your selections.

Allow for sufficient time so that you can stop the tape at unscheduled spots. Indicate at the beginning that you will stop at any time to answer questions.

Elicit enough information about the level of your audience members and their expectations to evaluate what parts will be the most useful.

Look for visual clues from the group as nonverbal requests for stopping the tape to discuss what was just seen.

Remember that it is more valuable to focus deeply and move slowly than to try to finish viewing an entire tape.

Consider giving a chart (see the next page) to people to help track Virginia's process. Otherwise, the content of the tape can involve people so completely that it distracts them from being aware of Virginia's process and learning from it.

Tracking a Session

These are areas that Virginia Satir covered or commented on during a session. Check each one as often as you observe her use of it. (You may also want to make a note of the content—what is being discussed.)

PROCESS

> Bridging
> The change process; transformation
> Communication: checking out for meaning; clarification of issues, words,
> > perceptions
> Decision making
> Differences and samenesses
> Directing

Discrepancies between words and behavior, words and feelings, the verbal and nonverbal
Empowering people
Enhancing self-esteem
Expectations, yearnings
Feelings
Growth
Healing
Making contact
Nonverbal communication commented on
Perceptions
Reducing tension, checking out comfort
Uniqueness

TECHNIQUES AND TOOLS

Acceptance
Dramatizing, story-telling
Exaggerating
Family Reconstruction and mini-reconstructions
Generalizing
Humor
Identification—similarity of feelings and situations
Interpreting
Metaphors
Modeling
Moving from one subject to another, one person to another
Normalizing; humanizing observations
Parts Party
Posing questions in an appropriate order
Reflecting
Reframing
Role playing
Sculpting
Timing
Touch
Use of the past—family chronology
Use of self
Validating

The Vulnerability Contract

"There are no solutions, only possibilities."

—*Virginia Satir*

This interesting and provocative format offers two people an opportunity to enhance their relationship.

Part One

First person:

> When I am feeling --- [worried],
>> what you will see is --- [I will become silent and withdraw].
>
> What I'd like from you is --- [ask me if I want to talk].

Second person:

> "I agree. However, when the time does not fit for me, I will let you know and make arrangements for a later time. If this is an emergency, I agree to respond immediately."
>
> So when I see --- [that you are silent and withdrawn],
>> what I will do is --- [ask if you want to talk].
>
> What I'd like from you is --- [tell me if you want to talk now or at a later time].

Note: This was presented by Bunny Duhl at a Satir meeting in Seattle, WA in 1980.

Part Two

The second person takes his or her turn and initiates the process as described above.

The contract is negotiable at any time by either person, either to amend the current one or to make a new one.

The Wire Experience

"Look at the past; don't stare at it."

—*Virginia Satir*

The purpose of this visual and kinesthetic experience is to give people the opportunity to see different periods of their lives and what their impact was.

Find wire that is flexible enough to be bent and twisted with some ease, yet sturdy enough to maintain the forms it is put into. You may use different colored wires. Cut them in nine-foot lengths.

Give each person one length. Ask each to see his or her wire as a representation of a certain period in his or her life, or let the wire represent the person's entire life span. For instance, it can be the teen years, the courtship period, the first years of marriage, the period following the birth of the person's first child, etc. The person bends and twists it as he or she thinks about what happened, how it felt, and how he or she coped with the differing experiences in that period of life.

After this has been done, ask people to share what they became aware of or learned about the period of life chosen, explaining and describing the bends and twists they made in their wires.

Books and Tapes by Virginia Satir

Grinder, John; Richard Bandler; and Virginia Satir. *Changing with Families.* Palo Alto, CA: Science and Behavior Books, 1976.

Satir, Virginia. *Conjoint Family Therapy,* Third Edition. Palo Alto, CA: Science and Behavior Books, 1987.

——. *Making Contact.* Millbrae, CA: Celestial Arts, 1976.

——. *The New Peoplemaking.* Palo Alto, CA: Science and Behavior Books, 1988.

——. *Old Sayings I Just Made Up.* Palo Alto, CA: Avanta Network, 1989.

——. *Self-Esteem.* Millbrae, CA: Celestial Arts, 1975.

——. *Thoughts and Feelings.* Palo Alto, CA: Avanta Network, 1989.

——. *Your Many Faces.* Millbrae, CA: Celestial Arts, 1978.

——; and Michele Baldwin. *Satir Step by Step: A Guide to Creating Change in Families.* Palo Alto, CA: Science and Behavior Books, 1983.

——; James Stachowiak; and Harvey A. Taschman. *Helping Families to Change.* New York: Jacob Aronson, 1977.

Schwab, Johanna; Michele Baldwin; Jane Gerber; Maria Gomori; and Virginia Satir. *The Satir Approach to Communication: A Workshop Manual.* Palo Alto, CA: Science and Behavior Books, 1989.

Audiotapes

Satir, Virginia. *The Memorial Series: Teachings of Virginia Satir.* Palo Alto, CA: Avanta Network, 1989.

Videotapes

Satir, Virginia. *Blended Family with a Troubled Boy.* Kansas City, MO: Golden Triad Films.

———. *The Essence of Change.* Kansas City, MO: Golden Triad Films.

———. *A Family at the Point of Growth.* Kansas City, MO: Golden Triad Films.

———. *Family Series I* [including a family interview, various Parts Parties, and Family Reconstruction]. Available through Dr. John Banmen, 11213 Canyon Crescent, N. Delta, BC V4E 2R6, Canada.

———. *Family Series III* [including Family Reconstruction]. Available through Dr. John Banmen, 11213 Canyon Crescent, N. Delta, BC V4E 2R6, Canada.

——— *Of Rocks and Flowers: Dealing with the Abuse of Children.* Kansas City, MO: Golden Triad Films.

———*A Step Along the Way: A Family with a Drug Problem.* Kansas City, MO: Golden Triad Films.

——— *Virginia Satir on Communication, Parts I and II.* Palo Alto, CA: Science and Behavior Books.

Index

The Avanta Network

The Avanta Network, founded by Virginia Satir in 1977, is an international training organization. Its worldwide members offer training to enhance self-esteem, increase interpersonal communication, and provide a process model for personal and organizational growth. Trainings deepen the participants' understanding of human systems and assist in the process of change.

Avanta-sponsored training events range from week-long to month-long seminars. Members are also available to lead workshops and introduce the Satir model to the public.

For more information, please contact the Avanta Network, 139 Forest Avenue, Palo Alto, CA 94301; telephone 415-327-1424.